W9-BZQ-686

The Little French ABC Coloring Book

by Anna Pomaska

Dover Publications, Inc.
New York

Published in Canada by General Publishing Company, Ltd., 30 Lesmill Road, Don Mills, Toronto, Ontario.

Published in the United Kingdom by Constable and Company, Ltd., 3 The Lanchesters, 162–164 Fulham Palace Road, London W6 9ER.

The Little French ABC Coloring Book is a new work, first published by Dover Publications, Inc., in 1991.

International Standard Book Number: 0-486-26812-8

Manufactured in the United States of America
Dover Publications, Inc., 31 East 2nd Street, Mineola, N.Y. **11501**

The Little French ABC Coloring Book

Avion

Bateau

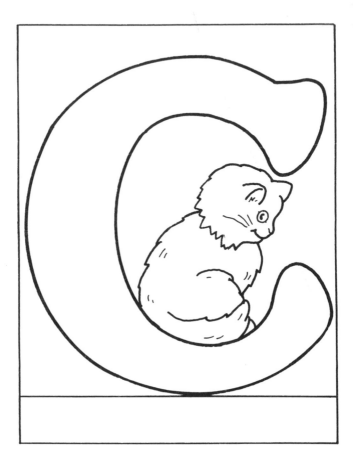

Chat

Dindon

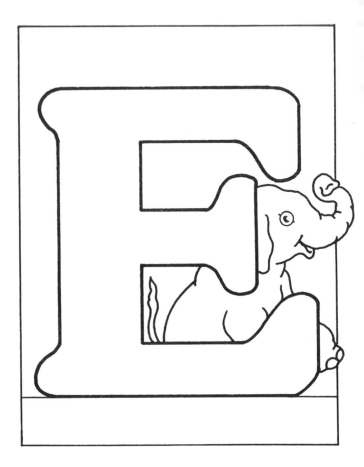

Éléphant

Fleur

Garçon

Hibou

Indien

24

Jardin

Kangourou

Livre

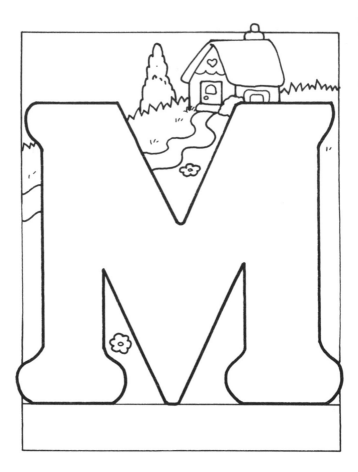

Maison

Nid

Oiseau

Papillon

Quatre

Roi

Soleil

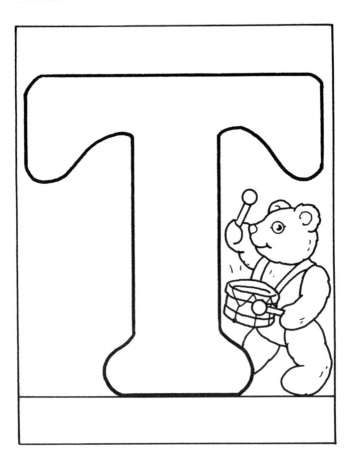

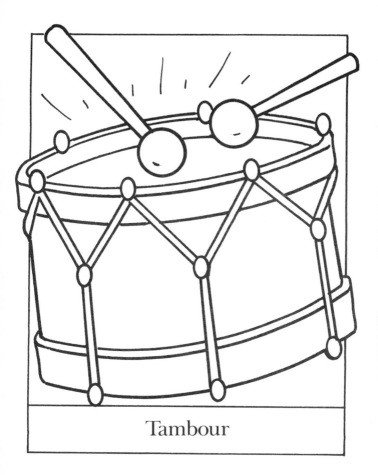

Tambour

Usine

Vache

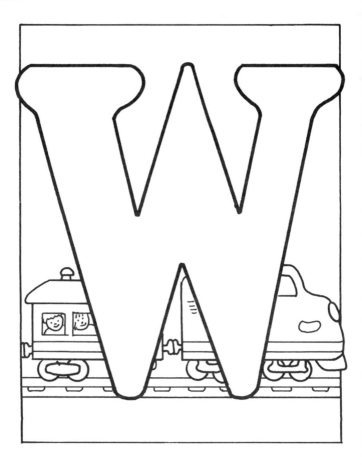

Wagon

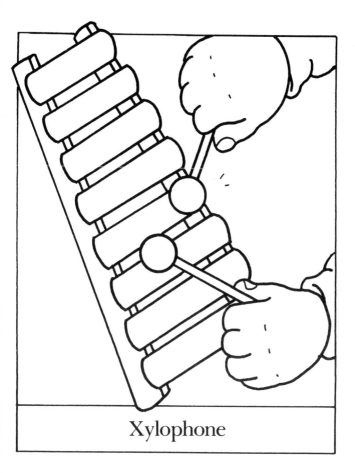

Xylophone

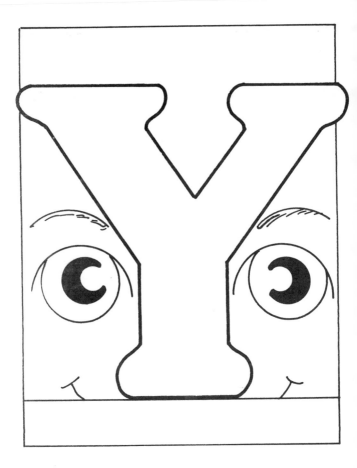

Yeux

Zèbre

Note

Whether children are studying French as a first or as a second language, they need to learn the alphabet and acquire useful vocabulary. One of the most enjoyable ways to help them remember both the letters of the alphabet and new words is by activity, especially in the form of coloring. The present book contains a full French alphabet keyed to essential everyday words, to names of animals and familiar objects, all charmingly illustrated by noted children's book designer Anna Pomaska. To help children "think in French," only the French words for the items illustrated appear in the main part of the book. On pages 61–62, the full word list is repeated, not only with English equivalents (forming a handy glossary) but also with the gender-indicating definite articles,* which ideally should be learned along with the words.

*When a French noun begins with a vowel, and for most words beginning with "h," the definite article is contracted to *l'*. The plural form of the definite article is *les*. Since the gender of a noun cannot be determined from the form of the article when *l'* or *les* is used, the following abbreviations have been used: MASC. (masculine) and FEM. (feminine).

French-English Word List

l'avion (MASC.)	the airplane
le bateau	the boat
le chat	the cat
le dindon	the turkey
l'éléphant (MASC.)	the elephant
la fleur	the flower
le garçon	the boy
le hibou	the owl
l'indien (MASC.)	the indian
le jardin	the garden
le kangourou	the kangaroo
le livre	the book
la maison	the house
le nid	the nest

l'oiseau (MASC.)	the bird
le papillon	the butterfly
quatre	four
le roi	the king
le soleil	the sun
le tambour	the drum
l'usine (FEM.)	the factory
la vache	the cow
le wagon	the railway car
le xylophone	the xylophone
les yeux (MASC.)	the eyes
le zèbre	the zebra